REPTILES ROCK!

INVESTIGATE!

KOMODO DRAGONS ARE THE LARGEST LIZARDS!

BY ELISE TOBLER

Enslow PUBLISHING

Please visit our website, www.enslow.com. For a free color catalog of all our high-quality books, call toll free 1-800-398-2504 or fax 1-877-980-4454.

Library of Congress Cataloging-in-Publication Data

Names: Tobler, Elise, 1970– author.
Title: Komodo dragons are the largest lizards! / Elise Tobler.
Description: New York : Enslow Publishing, [2021] | Series: Reptiles rock! | Includes index.
Identifiers: LCCN 2019050706 | ISBN 9781978518308 (library binding) | ISBN 9781978518285 (paperback) | ISBN 9781978518292 (six-pack) | ISBN 9781978518315 (ebook)
Subjects: LCSH: Komodo dragon—Juvenile literature.
Classification: LCC QL666.L29 T63 2021 | DDC 597.95/968—dc23
LC record available at https://lccn.loc.gov/2019050706

Published in 2021 by
Enslow Publishing
101 West 23rd Street, Suite #240
New York, NY 10011

Designer: Laura Bowen
Editor: Elise Tobler

Photo credits: Cover, p. 1 (Komodo dragon) Andrey Gudkov/Shutterstock.com; cover, pp. 1–32 (leaves border) Marina Solva/Shutterstock.com; pp. 4, 6 Wolfgang Kaehler/Contributor/LightRocket/Getty Images; p. 5 Rainer Lesniewski/Shutterstock.com; p. 7 Yulia Sundukova/Barcroft Image/Barcroft Media via Getty Images; p. 8 Lisa Larsen/Contributor/The LIFE Picture Collection/Getty Images; p. 9 Flickr upload bot/Wikimedia Commons; pp. 10–11 Eric Isselee/Shutterstock.com; p. 13 kkaplin/iStock/Getty Images Plus/Getty Images; p. 15 AYImages/E+/Getty Images; p. 17 (main) Barry Kusuma/Photolibrary/Getty Images Plus/Getty Images; pp. 17 (inset), 28 USO/iStock/Getty Images Plus; pp. 19 (main), 29 Andrey Gudkov/iStock/Getty Images Plus/Getty Images; p. 19 (inset) Donyanedomam/iStock/Getty Images; p. 20 Yui Mok – PA Images/Contributor/PA Images Getty Images Plus/Getty Images; p. 21 NurPhoto/Contributor/NurPhoto/Getty Images; p. 23 taarnes/iStock/Getty Images Plus/Getty Images; p. 24 Barry Kusuma/Taxi/Getty Images Plus/Getty Images; p. 25 (sign) Oliver J Davis Photography/Moment/Getty Images Plus/Getty Images; p. 25 (island) Afriandi/Moment/Getty Images; p. 27 Andrew Parsons – PA Images/Contributor/PA Images/Getty Images.

Portions of this work were originally authored by Kathleen Connors and published as *Komodo Dragons*. All new material this edition authored by Elise Tobler.

Printed in the United States of America

CPSIA compliance information: Batch #BS20ENS: For further information contact Enslow Publishing, New York, New York, at 1-800-398-2504.

CONTENTS

Words in the glossary appear in **bold** type the first time they are used in the text.

DRAGONS OF UNUSUAL SIZE

Komodo dragons are the largest lizards in the world! They were first called "land crocodiles." In the wild, they live in Komodo National Park in Indonesia, a country made up of islands in Southeast Asia.

The average length of a male Komodo dragon is 8 to 9 feet (2.4 to 2.7 m), but some as long as 10 feet (3 m) have been recorded. Female Komodo dragons are usually 6 feet (1.8 m) long. The largest Komodo dragon ever found weighed 366 pounds (166 kg)!

GET THE FACTS!

In 1926, American W. Douglas Burden traveled to Indonesia to capture Komodo dragons. He wanted the world to see how amazing they were. His journey inspired the movie *King Kong*, about the journey to capture a huge, never-before-seen ape.

Komodo National Park, shown in green, is made up of many islands.

HERE THERE BE DRAGONS

Komodo dragons can be many different colors, from green and gray to blue and orange. Their bodies are covered in scales called osteoderms. These scales are hard like armor and make Komodo dragons difficult to bite or hurt. The older the lizard gets, the harder its scales become.

The tail of a Komodo dragon is usually as long as its body and is one big muscle. Komodo dragons can use their tail for balance or defense. They use it to knock over predators. Mostly, the only predators of Komodo dragons are other Komodo dragons!

Komodo dragons often wrestle to test their strength.

GET THE FACTS!

Komodo dragons originally came from Australia. **Fossil** records show that Komodo dragons traveled to Indonesia about 900,000 years ago, walking and swimming to reach the islands. They vanished from Australia 50,000 years ago, when humans began to arrive.

HOME SWEET HOME

Komodo dragons love hot weather, so the Lesser Sunda Islands of Indonesia where they live are perfect for them. The Lesser Sunda Islands are north of Australia and are called an **archipelago**. These islands have jungles, beaches, and volcanoes.

Komodo dragons are good swimmers!

Komodo dragons have done so well on these islands because there aren't any larger carnivores, or meat eaters, there. This means the Komodo dragons are in charge! They love to lay on warm beaches and also enjoy the forests. Sometimes, they dig burrows, or holes, to escape the heat. They will also take over burrows made by other animals.

GET THE FACTS!

Komodo dragons sometimes swim between islands to find better food. They like familiar surroundings and don't stay away from home for long.

SMELLING WITH A TONGUE

Komodo dragons have a very strong sense of smell, but their nose doesn't do all the work. Like the tongues of snakes and other reptiles, the tongue of the Komodo dragon is one of its most important smelling tools.

When Komodo dragons flick their tongue into the air, it brings back smells that they can "taste." The tongue is split, which means if the "taste" is stronger on the right side, a Komodo dragon knows what it's looking for is to the right.

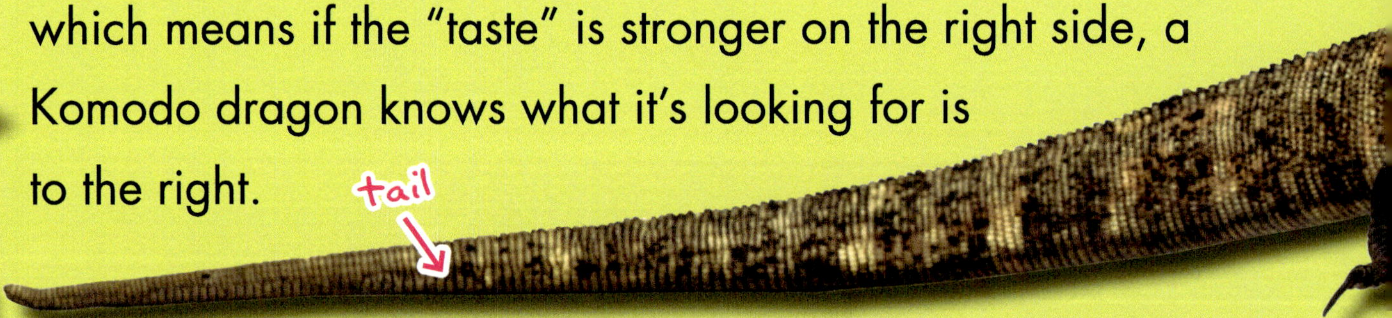

GET THE FACTS!

Komodo dragons have a **metabolism** that is more like that of mammals. This means they digest, or break down, food quickly. This helps them move quickly so they can hunt bigger animals.

Komodo dragons have forked tongues and very long tails.

DINERS, DRAGONS, AND DIVES

Komodo dragons are carnivores. That means they eat meat. They will hunt very big animals, such as water buffalo and deer. They will also hunt smaller animals, like pigs. Often, they feed on carrion, or dead animals, left behind by other animals.

Komodo dragons have big **appetites**. They can eat as much as 80 percent of their body weight in one sitting! Komodo dragons will also often eat bones and hooves, but they spit these out later in the form of a pellet, much like owls do.

GET THE FACTS!

Sometimes, adult Komodo dragons will eat baby Komodo dragons. To **camouflage** themselves, baby Komodo dragons will roll themselves in poop! This makes them smell like something an adult doesn't want to eat.

AMBUSH!

Komodo dragons can move pretty fast considering how large they are. They can run anywhere from 10 to 13 miles (16 to 20 km) per hour. But their speed isn't often used when they hunt. Komodo dragons like to hide, wait, and ambush their **prey**. Ambush means they jump out and surprise the animal!

Even if the prey escapes, it's doomed. The bite of a Komodo dragon contains venom, or poison made in its body. It kills the prey. Komodo dragons use their sense of smell to find the body.

GET THE FACTS!

Komodo dragons have 60 tiny teeth, and each one is **serrated**. A Komodo dragon may go through five sets of teeth in its lifetime, as each set falls out when the teeth get too worn to work well.

Komodo dragons have a dangerous bite, but they don't commonly attack people.

PLAYING DEFENSE

Komodo dragons don't have many predators to fear, except humans. Komodo dragons tend to fear other Komodo dragons, especially when it comes time to find a **mate**.

When they feel they are in danger, Komodo dragons can throw up the contents of their stomach. This is probably alarming to the animal attacking it, but it also makes the Komodo dragon lighter and allows it to run away faster. Komodo dragons are also large enough that they can knock into predators and tip them over.

Komodo dragons can climb trees in search of food or safety.

GET THE FACTS!

Komodo dragons' speed on land isn't used when hunting. But it helps them get away from anything attacking them!

FAMILY MATTERS

Komodo dragons tend to live **solitary** lives, except when it's time to find a mate. Male Komodo dragons fight each other to see who is the strongest.

Female Komodo dragons can lay up to 30 eggs at one time. They make **decoy** nests to keep the eggs safe while the babies grow. Female Komodo dragons can also **reproduce** without male Komodo dragons. This is called asexual reproduction. The conditions around the females have to be just right for them to have babies without males around.

The strongest Komodo dragon gets to choose his mate!

GET THE FACTS!

Female Komodo dragons use three different kinds of nests when they are hiding their eggs: ground nests, hillside nests, and mound nests already built by birds.

BABY DRAGONS

Mother Komodo dragons don't wait around after their babies are born. When babies hatch, or come out of their shell, they're on their own. Baby Komodo dragons use an **egg tooth** to help them crack the eggshell. **Instinct** sends them into trees, where they are safer from larger Komodo dragons that may eat them.

GET THE FACTS!

Female Komodo dragons don't have babies every year. Being a mother is hard work, and Komodo dragons can take a "rest" year to build themselves back up from laying such a large number of eggs the year before.

Once they hatch, baby Komodo dragons eat geckos, crickets, grasshoppers, and beetles. When the Komodo dragons are about 4 years old, they start living on the ground full-time.

When baby Komodo dragons hatch, they climb trees and start looking for food.

SOLAR POWERED

Like other lizards, Komodo dragons are cold-blooded, which means their bodies are the same temperature as their surroundings. Komodo dragons need to find ways to heat up, which is why they like living where it's warm. Laying on sun-warmed rocks allows them to warm up as they need to.

Komodo dragons are unique in how they use their energy. They are more like mammals than other lizards are, as they are able to use more of the energy from the food they consume. This makes them faster than other cold-blooded reptiles might be.

Komodo dragons love to sun themselves on rocks to stay warm.

GET THE FACTS!

Mammals and birds are warm-blooded, which means they can keep their body at a steady temperature, no matter their surroundings. Lizards, reptiles, and amphibians cannot do this. They need to get warm in the sun.

DUNGEONS AND KOMODO DRAGONS

People often try to illegally sell Komodo dragons. In 2019, one group tried to take 41 young Komodo dragons out of Indonesia. It was guessed that each Komodo dragon could sell for $35,000! The Komodo dragons were taken from their home on the island of Flores.

This Komodo dragon is at home on Flores Island, Indonesia.

Komodo dragons do best in their own environment—the natural place where they were born. They don't live well in cities, except for zoos where people know how to care for them. But the world is growing harder for Komodo dragons to live in.

Komodo National Park

GET THE FACTS!

Komodo National Park was founded in 1980, in part to help Komodo dragons live in the wild. Efforts have expanded to include land and sea. This helps the Komodo dragons stay safe.

DRAGONS ON DISPLAY

Zoos across the world have Komodo dragons to study them and help them reproduce. In 2010, the Los Angeles Zoo hatched 22 baby Komodo dragons!

Komodo dragons in zoos are often tamer than those in the wild. They can learn who their keepers are. Komodo dragons in captivity may become fatter than those in the wild because they are fed more regularly. Komodo dragons have also shown that they know how to play. They like to push objects around and enjoy shaking cups, blankets, and drink cans.

Komodo dragons cannot be kept as pets. See one at the zoo!

GET THE FACTS!

"Captivity" means the state of being kept and not being in the wild. For animals, this often means living at a zoo or animal park.

FUTURE KOMODOS

Scientists say there are about 5,700 Komodo dragons living in the wild. They are considered a vulnerable and endangered species, which means their kind of animal could die out. Because their numbers are so small, all Komodo dragons could be lost from illness, loss of habitat, **poaching**, or a volcanic eruption on their home islands.

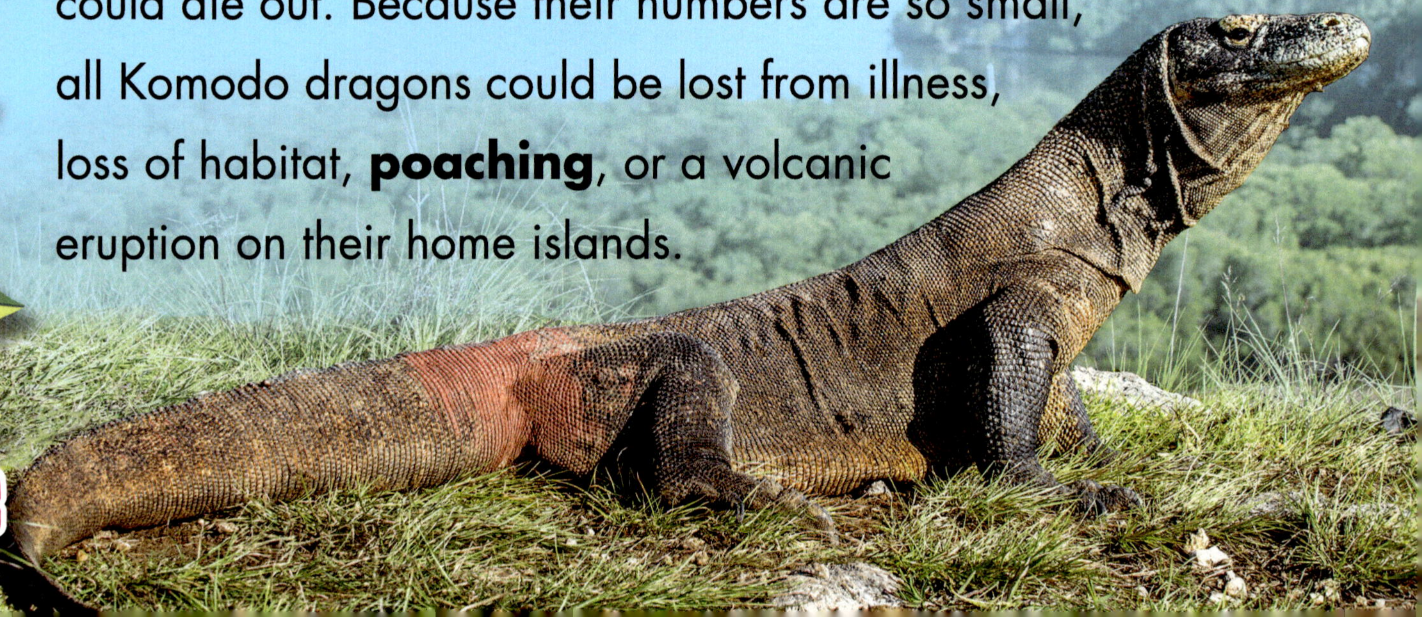

In 2019, park officials considered closing Komodo National Park. So many people come to see the Komodo dragons that it may be harmful to them. Komodo dragons are protected by Indonesia, but they still face challenges to survive.

GET THE FACTS!

"Protected" means people are not allowed to hunt, capture, or sell Komodo dragons in any way. However, this hasn't stopped people from trying to catch them.

GLOSSARY

appetite A need for food.
archipelago A group of islands.
camouflage To blend in with one's surroundings.
decoy Something used to trick someone or redirect their attention.
egg tooth A hard, white part on the mouth of a baby reptile that is used for breaking out of an egg and is later lost.
fossil The marks or remains of plants and animals that formed over thousands or millions of years.
instinct A way of behaving, thinking, or feeling that is not learned.
mate One of two animals that comes together to make babies.
metabolism The chemical processes by which a plant or animal uses food and water to grow and heal and to make energy.
poach To catch or kill an animal illegally.
prey An animal that is hunted by other animals for food.
reproduce When an animal creates another creature just like itself.
serrated Having a row of small points along the side, like a saw.
solitary Tending to live or spend time alone.

FOR MORE INFORMATION

Books

Davidson, John. *Komodo Dragons for Kids*. Scotts Valley, CA: CreateSpace Publishing, 2015.

Ganeri, Anita. *The Story of the Komodo Dragon*. Portsmouth, NH: Heinemann, 2016.

Goodman, Keith. *All About Reptiles for Kids*. Sacramento, CA: Great Little, 2018.

Websites

National Geographic
kids.nationalgeographic.com/animals/reptiles/komodo-dragon/
Check out National Geographic's page on Komodo dragons!

San Diego Zoo
animals.sandiegozoo.org/animals/komodo-dragon
The San Diego Zoo has great photos and facts about Komodo dragons.

Publisher's note to educators and parents: Our editors have carefully reviewed these websites to ensure that they are suitable for students. Many websites change frequently, however, and we cannot guarantee that a site's future contents will continue to meet our high standards of quality and educational value. Be advised that students should be closely supervised whenever they access the internet.

INDEX